ean on me

So hold my nana,

let me take you to

r a father and a friend
g that the ... will end

a friend of mine

He's waiting just to

ease your troubled mind

Presented to

_____

From

_____

Date

_____

A note to you:

_____

_____

_____

_____

_____

A friend loves at all times.

PROVERBS 17:17

J. COUNTRYMAN
Nashville, Tennessee

LEAN ON ME

KIRK FRANKLIN

with Robert J. Morgan

ACKNOWLEDGEMENTS

"Can't You Hear Him Cryin' Out?" From Robert J. Morgan, *Real Stories for the Soul* (Nashville: Thomas Nelson, © 2000), pp. 293-295.

"You Don't Have to Worry." Adapted from the article "Gifts From My Father" by Curt Bradford in *Experiencing God* magazine, December 1995, pp. 16-17.

Published by J. Countryman®, a division of Thomas Nelson, Inc., Nashville, Tennessee 37214

"Lean On Me" words and music by Kirk Franklin, © 1998 Lilly Mack Music/Kerrion Publishing (Adm. By Lilly Mack Music) (BMI).

Project editor: Jenny Baumgartner

Designed by Koechel Peterson & Associates, Inc., Minneapolis, Minnesota

ISBN: 0-8499-5615-X

Printed and bound in the United States of America

www.jcountryman.com

A Note From Kirk

It is a blessing to be able to help someone who has been a good friend and a blessing to you. I am experiencing this in my life with a friend who supported me several years ago. At that time, I had a child out of wedlock, and a lot of my church friends had turned their backs on me because they were embarrassed by my situation. It was a very painful time, and I needed someone to show me in a right, loving way that I still had God's grace.

I felt so ashamed of myself that I walked with my head down in church. My mother (who had adopted me) was about seventy-eight years old, and she was a very strong church-going woman. She wasn't happy that I didn't marry the mother of my child, so she put me out when I was nineteen. It was the Fourth of July.

I didn't have any relatives, so I slept on a friend's floor that night. The next day, I asked another friend if I could stay with him. I continued to move from place to place—eleven times in all, just kind of living out of my car. Then finally, one friend said to me, "However long it takes you to get on your feet, you can stay with my mother and me." It was a wonderful offer. Not only did he let me stay with him, but I didn't have to sleep on the floor. He let me have his bed. A short time later, my mother died, and she willed everything to me. She blessed me with a house, and she had some money saved that helped me get back on my feet.

It's funny how God orchestrated my situation. This friend opened his home and let me stay with him, and at the time, he was in a homosexual lifestyle. Even though he knew that I did not agree with his lifestyle, he let me stay. Now my friend is dying of AIDS, and I'm able to return the favor of friendship. I'm able to help him buy medicine. I also helped him and his mom buy a car.

He and I have talked about his lifestyle, and I've been able to minister to him in the spirit of love, but still in truth—the way Jesus would have done. I'm still there for him as much as I can be. Financially and otherwise, I am loaning him my shoulder. It is a true blessing.

I pray that this book will inspire you to be a vessel of blessing to others, and may the words in these pages encourage you in those times when you, too, need someone to lean on.

KIRK FRANKLIN

riends are there to catch you when you fall.

Here's my shoulder;

Here's my shoulder,

You can lean on me.

"Lean On Me"

Lean On Me

WORDS AND MUSIC BY KIRK FRANKLIN

This is for the little child with no father
For that man that doesn't have a place to stay
And for that little boy living with AIDS
You can lean on me

There's a man
Standing on the corner
He has no home, he has no food
And his blue skies are gone
Can't you hear him crying out

And there's a girl
Searching for a father and a friend
Praying that the storm someday will end
But instead of walkin' away
Open up your heart and say

CHORUS:

I am here
You don't have to worry, I can see your tears
I'll be there in a hurry when you call
Friends are there to catch you when you fall

Here's my shoulder, you can lean on me

There's a child who is sick and begging to be free
But there is no cure for his disease
He looks up to his mother as she holds his hand
Prayin' that someday the sun will shine again
And the pain, pain will end, come on

CHORUS

Tell me how can I, how can I love Jesus
When I've never seen His face
Yet I see you dying
And I turn and walk away

So hold my hand, let me take you to a friend of mine
He's waiting just to ease your troubled mind
He loves you more than you'll ever know
Instead of walkin' away, open up
Open up your heart and say

CHORUS

You're my friend, but you're also my brother
Hallelujah

STANDING ON THE CORNER

"My congregation is always standing on the corner, waiting for me," says Chuck Snow. "They pay for my services in advance, and I have the benefit of preaching most of my sermons sitting down."

For over twenty-five years, Chuck has been a bus driver with the public transit system in Atlanta, Georgia. On the "job," he ministers to his passengers from the driver's seat, offering both a listening ear and words of compassion. It's a calling that he dearly loves.

As a young man, however, Chuck wasn't sure what he wanted to do with his life. Following a term in the military, he went to a Christian college and planned to enter the youth ministry. But the Lord seemed to lead him in another direction, and eventually he was hired as a bus driver in Atlanta. He soon realized God had placed him in a ministry just as strategic as any missionary's.

"I love people," says Chuck, "especially young people. I do a lot of listening. I get all excited when someone is on the bus and they want to talk. Sometimes all it takes is a question from me and a flicker of concern, and everything comes spilling out. I like to say I've got my Ph.D. in listening."

Chuck's regular passengers know they can call him at home when they're in need of advice or prayer. "I don't try to knock them over with a five-point outline," says Chuck. "I'm not a preacher, but I try to listen, to be a friend. And when appropriate, I seem to know how to get the Scripture across."

Recently, a young man climbed aboard, and Chuck could tell he was troubled about something. He was Chuck's only passenger, so it wasn't hard to strike up a conversation. Soon the young man was weeping, and as they rolled down boulevards and crossed intersections, Chuck quoted Scripture and advised him with precious truths from God's Word. Before the man left, they prayed together.

Chuck's passengers don't always realize it, but when they step into his bus, they are entering holy ground.

Open Up Your Heart

As soon as the song "Lean On Me" was released, Philip Bray started getting phone calls. "The phone was ringing off the wall. Everyone was saying, 'When I heard 'Lean on Me,' I thought of SafeHouse.'"

Phillip, the executive director of SafeHouse Outreach Ministries of Atlanta, Georgia, immediately purchased the CD. "When I heard the song, I started weeping," he says. "It hit home. It kind of explains our purpose."

In 1983, Phillip founded SafeHouse, and today the ministry offers church services, food, clothes, hope, healing, and more to those who have fallen through the cracks of traditional churches. Prior to 1983, however, Phillip himself was in need of such help.

Despite growing up in a parsonage, the son of a preacher, he strayed from the grace of God during his younger years. "I began drinking and drugging," he says. "Especially cocaine. I developed a thousand-dollar-a-day habit, and I was in real bad shape. I got involved with organized crime—the Dixie Mafia—to pay for my habit, and I was doing everything, and I mean everything. I didn't just go from bad to worse, I went from worse to worst.

"Then one night I came home stoned after a party and turned on the television. There was my cousin, Billy Watson, on a religious program. I couldn't believe it. I idolized Billy. He owned about fifty nightclubs across the country. He was involved in a lot of bad things, but he had a lot of money and was very successful, very powerful. I admired him because of that. He always wore a lot of jewelry and was very gaudy, a very proud man, but I thought of him as the most successful person I knew.

"Well, there he was on television, talking about how Jesus Christ had changed his life. Every time I'd ever seen him, he was high or drunk, but there he was—sober and sharing his testimony.

"I was curious, so I listened. But I decided he was scamming, just doing it for the money. Then I found out that Billy would be speaking at my dad's church the following Sunday night, and I was furious—I thought he was just trying to get money out of the church."

At his mother's pleading, Philip nevertheless decided

to attend that Sunday evening to hear Billy's presentation. Philip was stoned when he took his seat on the back pew, and he was still angry. But that night Billy could hardly talk for crying. He kept saying, "I once was in bondage, but now I'm free. I tried getting off drugs and alcohol on my own, but I couldn't. Jesus is the only way to freedom."

On the back row, a sobered Philip listened intently. His anger melted away, and the message took hold of his heart. "I took him up on it," said Philip. "That evening I gave my own heart to Jesus, and Jesus set me free."

We are not saviors, but we can help others toward faith. This means not only loving them while they're still in the mire, but loving them out of it.

ELISABETH ELLIOT

And there's a girl
  Searching for a father and a friend

  Praying that the storm will someday end
  But instead of walking away

  Open up your heart and say....

  Lean on me

KIRK FRANKLIN
"Lean On Me"

AND THERE'S A GIRL . . .

When Philip Bray gave his life to Jesus on a Sunday night in his father's church, he had a lot of ground to make up. Everyone was happy for him, yet no one trusted him enough to give him a job. But the Lord had a job for him.

One day a friend named Al Palmquist challenged him to go into the streets, witnessing to prostitutes. Phillip says, "Al challenged me to approach prostitutes about the Lord and to share Christ with them. I asked him to go with me, but he had a plane to catch. So I called a friend named Keith, a street-level dope dealer who had gotten saved, and said, 'Let's go talk to hookers about Jesus.'"

Keith said, "I'll go on one condition, that I bring my gun."

That night Philip and Keith (accompanied by Smith & Wesson) wandered through the streets, seeking to witness but having little success. The prostitutes thought they were crazy, and discouragement began to set in.

"Keith," Philip said, "I don't think I'm called to a ministry of rejection. Why don't we pray about this. We forgot to pray before we started."

So the two men joined hands on the sidewalk and prayed a simple prayer, asking God's blessings on their efforts. As they finished, a teenage girl crossed the street in high heels and a short dress. Approaching them, she said, "Hi, guys, what's happening?

"I guess you're happening," they said. "How's business?"

"Not too good. I don't think I can feed my child tonight."

The two men had never thought of a prostitute as a loving, caring mother, as someone willing to sell her body to take care of her child. They began asking her questions.

"Are you guys cops?" she asked, tensing.

"No," said Philip. "We just care about you."

"Nobody cares about anybody here in the street," she said.

"Surely your parents care about you."

"Let me tell you about my parents," the girl said bitterly. "At age nine, my father pimped me out to pay his poker debts. By age twelve, I was pregnant. My mother threw me out of the house, and since then I've just been trying to survive for me and my kid."

"Well," said Philip, "God cares about you." And he began sharing the Scriptures with her, telling her about Christ and reading from Psalm 46. "We're just two old dope dealers turned hope dealers," they said. "We were wandering around here, and you crossed our path. God saw you and your need. He sent you over to talk to us."

The girl, weeping now, said, "I just prayed today to the God of my grandma to send someone to help me. I know that my grandmother knew the real God, and I told God that if He didn't help me today, I was going to kill my child and myself tonight."

The two men prayed with the girl, led her to Christ, and got her off the streets.

"When I started SafeHouse Outreach Ministries in Atlanta," says Philip, "our primary focus was on winning prostitutes to Christ. Today SafeHouse is reaching five hundred to one thousand people a day in urban Atlanta. And it all started with her."

∽

We must not come to our dear Lord at all,

unless we can call him Friend;

and we may not call him Friend unless

we also call the poor our friends.

JOHN MASON NEALE

COME ON

Her goal was twenty-six miles long, plus another 385 yards. Wanting to encourage a fellow runner, Joanie McLeod decided to enter the St. Louis marathon. It was an ambitious goal, so Joanie started training at once. As the race neared, her friend Robin felt an unusual urge to pray for her, and on the week of the run, Robin decided to make something for Joanie to carry in the race. This would be highly unusual because marathoners strip away everything that might slow them down. But Robin felt compelled to give her something anyway.

But what? Robin searched through her booklet of small cross-stitched Scripture verse patterns, looking for one about strength, running, or athletics. But her eye kept coming back to a tiny fragment from Exodus 4:18: *Go in peace.* And that is the one she cross-stitched. Then, slipping a small safety pin through it, she stuck it in a card to Joanie with a brief note.

When Joanie returned from St. Louis, she told Robin all about the trip and about her experiences during the marathon. Then she pulled out the cap she had worn in the race with the little Scripture tag hanging from it.

"What you don't know," said Joanie, "is that the night before I left for St. Louis, a relative called me. My cousin had committed suicide. Your verse prompted me to pray, 'Lord, You are so good. In my confusion, help me live in peace.' I decided to go on to St. Louis, for the sake of my fellow runner who, in turn, needed *my* encouragement."

"Since then," Joanie said, "that little cross-stitched verse has held deep significance for me. Whenever I see it, it immediately takes me back to that time, that place, those simple but powerful truths that I asked the Lord to NOT let me soon forget."

∞

HERE'S MY SHOULDER

A tall, gangling teenager, all arms and legs, Richard Van Kluyve has a smile as big as the summer sun. Not long ago, Richard was traveling in California with his church youth group, but the trip was stopped when he was called aside for a message. His older brother Eric, who was newly married, had suffered a brain aneurysm back in Tennessee.

Feeling ill at work, Eric had stepped into the restroom. Another worker had found him unconscious on the floor, and his chances of survival were very slim. Eric was Richard's only sibling, and the two brothers were unusually close.

Richard, hearing the news, slumped onto the park bench, his face in his hands, tears coming. "I've got to see my brother," he said. "He can't die until I get there."

Richard's youth group rallied around him, crying and praying and singing, and he soaked up their love like a sponge. Then he left for the airport to return home.

Eric was being kept alive by machines until Richard arrived. Friends from church met him at the airport and drove him to the hospital. When he arrived, the lobby, the hallways, and even the intensive care unit were filled with other members of his church. A sea of faces parted as he entered his brother's cubicle. They withdrew discreetly as he knelt by Eric's bedside and said "good-bye." His parents and Eric's young wife stood near-at-hand, weeping.

The days that followed were marked by hundreds of hugs, an ocean of love, and thousands of prayers for Richard and his family. A line of friends stood four-hours deep at the funeral home to pay their respects. Church members brought food, answered phones, laundered clothes, arranged rides, and, later, helped pay the bills.

Today Richard is in Bible college, preparing for the ministry. The memories of those days are still painful, for the loss of an only brother and best friend created a void no one else can fill. But the strength and support of his friends bore him through it, and bear him still.

"I had a thousand shoulders during those days," he said. "I leaned on every one of them. Every hug gave me strength."

Jesus was busy. He was popular.
Some people were trying to get his autograph,
and others were trying to kill Him.
He had his crew around Him,
but He always took time out for people
that touched His heart. He would make
the world stop just for that one person.

KIRK FRANKLIN

A friend is one who walks in when the rest of the world walks out.

WALTER WINCHELL

His nightmares began each day when he awoke. James Stegalls was nineteen. He was in Vietnam. Though he carried a small Gideon New Testament in his shirt pocket, he couldn't bring himself to read it. His buddies were cut down around him, terror was building within him, and God seemed far away. His twentieth birthday passed, then his twenty-first, but he felt he couldn't go on.

On February 26, 1968, he prayed for it all to end, and his heart told him he would die before dusk. Sure enough, his base came under attack that day and Jim heard a rocket coming straight toward him. Three seconds to live, he told himself, then two, then . . .

A friend shoved him into a grease pit, and he waited for the rocket to explode, but there was only a surreal silence. The fuse had malfunctioned.

For five hours James knelt in that pit, and finally his quivering hand reached into his shirt pocket and took out his Testament. Beginning with Matthew, he continued through the first eighteen chapters.

"When I read Matthew 18:19–20," he said, "I somehow knew things would be all right."

Long after Jim returned home, he visited his wife's grandmother, Mrs. Harris. She told him about a night years before when she had awakened in terror. Knowing Jim was in Vietnam, she had sensed he was in trouble. She began praying for God to spare his life. Unable to kneel because of arthritis, she lay prone on the floor, praying and reading her Bible all night.

Just before dawn she read Matthew 18:19–20: *If two of you agree on earth concerning anything that they ask, it will be done for them by My Father in heaven. For where two or three are gathered together in My name, I am in the midst of them.*

After she read those verses, she immediately called her Sunday school teacher, who got out of bed and came to Mrs. Harris' house. Together they claimed the Lord's promise as they prayed for Jim until they felt reassured by God's peace.

Having told Jim the story, Mrs. Harris opened her Bible to show him where she had marked the passage.

In the margin were the words: *Jim, February 26, 1968.*

How can I love Jesus

When I've never seen His face?. . .

So hold my hand,

Let me take you to a friend of mine

He's waiting just to ease your troubled mind

He loves you more than you'll ever know

KIRK FRANKLIN

"Lean On Me"

HE'S WAITING JUST TO EASE YOUR TROUBLED MIND

Willy was in trouble. Homeless. Drinking. Drugging. Sleeping under a bridge or wherever he could. One Wednesday night he made his way to SafeHouse Outreach Ministries in downtown Atlanta, Georgia. The regular speaker at SafeHouse on Wednesday night is Joe McUtchen, and week after week he teaches and preaches the Gospel of Jesus Christ.

Over several Wednesday nights, as Willy listened attentively, the message took root. Seeing his progress, SafeHouse placed Willy in a Christian drug rehab program in Tampa, Florida. Some months later, Willy called Joe to invite him to his graduation from the program.

"Willy, I just can't make it," said Joe apologetically, "but tell me how life's treating you."

"Well, Joe, when I got here they asked me a lot about my addictions, and they helped me through withdrawals. They talked to me a lot about God, and they tested my job skills. When they found out I used to be a master chef, they called around and got me a job at the Ritz-Carlton."

"The Ritz-Carlton!"

"Yeah, and in my rehab program I learned that I should do everything with all my heart, like I was doing it for God. So—would you believe it?—I'm head chef at the Ritz-Carlton. But Joe . . ."

"Yes, Willy?"

"I'd like to come back to SafeHouse in Atlanta on a Wednesday night and give my testimony. I'd like to tell the guys what Christ can do, and how your messages helped change my life."

"That'd be great, Willy," said Joe. "Let's plan that real soon. And when you come to town, Judy and I would like for you to stay with us. No need to pay for a room."

There was a pause on the line, then Willy said, "That's not necessary, Joe. When I come to Atlanta, there's already a room waiting for me."

"Oh?"

"Yeah, Joe. I'll be staying at the Ritz."

HOW CAN I LOVE JESUS...?

The laws of God are like Russian nesting dolls, those wooden dolls of decreasing sizes that can be placed inside each other until only the largest is visible for display. There are hundreds of commands and directives in the Bible, but they all can be stacked inside the Ten Commandments. The Ten Commandments, in turn, can be neatly stowed and stored in our Lord's two Great Commandments, given in Matthew 22:35-40:

Jesus said to him, "'You shall love the Lord your God with all your heart, with all your soul, and with all your mind.' This is the first and great commandment. And the second is like it: 'You shall love your neighbor as yourself.' On these two commandments hang all the Law and the Prophets."

It all comes down to *Love*. God is telling us that the person who truly *loves* will, as a matter of course, keep and obey all the other commands in the Bible.

That clears up the confusion we've created about this little word. Love isn't primarily an emotion, but an attitude. Love is a durable, rugged verb that God demonstrated to us by giving us His Son to die on the cross. He left the highest heavens to die the ugliest death in order to meet our deepest needs.

In turn, we demonstrate our love toward others by finding and meeting needs in their lives, by treating them with compassion, patience, dignity, and honesty. We give them our time, our friendship, our means, and our shoulders to lean on.

Remember, that which you give freely to others will be given back to you in greater measure. It's a rule of God's kingdom!

Give, and it will be given to you: good measure, pressed down,

shaken together, and running over will be put into your bosom.

For with the same measure that you use, it will be measured

back to you.

LUKE 6:38

We are not judges who determine how grace should be handed out. Grace is grace, and if you are in need, then I am there to meet the need. God is not looking at how we handle the situation as much as He is looking at the heart that is giving it.

KIRK FRANKLIN

I Can See Your Tears

Bob and Carolyn Thomas once served as missionaries in Papua New Guinea. Among Bob's stories is this one:

"It was Sunday morning in the village. I started a fire in the fireplace while Carolyn fixed cheese omelets. As soon as I finished breakfast, I turned on our shortwave and picked up the Kentucky Derby on a U.S. station. It was exciting to hear, but afterwards I was flooded with home-sick memories of our springtime family ritual of watching the Derby together. I was surprised when the tears came.

"Looking back, I realize the Lord was preparing my heart for another sorrow. A village leader had just died. I planned to spend Sunday on the mountain where my village friends were mourning, so I hiked to the top of the mountain and joined my adopted village brothers. In this area of New Guinea, people kick the bamboo-woven walls off the house of someone who dies. It is a release for their enormous grief. The walls of this dead man's house had already been kicked off and nailed back three times.

"I felt so sorry for them. I thought again how I missed

my family back home. I couldn't hold them back, so a few tears trickled down. Then I heard whispers through the crowd, 'Lala siacma' ('The Whiteskin cries!'). Suddenly two men leapt on top of me, knocking my glasses off. They held me tightly, and the whole crowd wailed.

"Afterwards they told me they didn't think Whiteskins cried. In their culture, if someone is sad and only cries a little, they jump on him to help the mourner cry hard and get it all out. They say it is no good if the sorrow stays inside you and kills you. I thought, 'Wow, they are wiser than we are about mourning.'"

Bob later said that the tribe had seen missionaries before. Several had visited them and even lived among them. But having never seen a missionary weep, they thought "Whiteskins" were incapable of tears. But now the story went out over the mountains that the Whiteskins really love us, they share our deep sorrow, they do care after all.

∞

God doesn't always bless you
with things just for you,
but He blesses you
with things for His kingdom.
God is interested in kingdom building
more than superstar building.

KIRK FRANKLIN

This is a very desensitized society that we live in,

but there are still people out there

who have the heart of God,

who are anxious to come to the rescue.

Every blue moon you find them, but they are there.

They still have morals and ethics

that Christ would smile at.

When we find those people we should

embrace them as saints and brothers.

KIRK FRANKLIN

YOU DON'T HAVE TO WORRY

Curt Bradford, a pastor in Charleston, South Carolina, remembers his seventh Christmas Eve. He crawled into bed that night so excited he couldn't get his eyes to close. Pretending to be asleep, he lay there until he was sure his parents were snoring. Then, around 2 a.m., he crept downstairs.

There under the Christmas trees were his presents. A drum set beckoned him to play it then and there, but he didn't dare. But he found other gifts he could play with. A cowboy outfit, a set of six-shooters, a puppet. Filled with excitement, he emptied his stocking, began eating the candy, the apple, the orange . . . But suddenly, hearing a noise, he turned and saw his Dad looking sternly down at him.

For a fleeting moment, Curt was afraid, but his dad broke into a smile, settled himself in the recliner, and listened while Curt showed him everything, explaining how the six-shooters worked and how the puppet moved its mouth.

Sleep soon came over him, and his dad picked him up, carried him upstairs, and tenderly tucked him into bed.

The next morning they had a wonderful Christmas, but, Curt said, "I will never forget that Christmas Eve."

The years flew by, and on another memorable Christmas, Curt found himself again at his father's side. This time the older man lay paralyzed from an automobile accident and was weak from cancer. Treatments, therapy, and experimental drugs had left him weighing less than one hundred pounds. Despite his pain, he asked if Curt would dress him so he could watch the family open presents. He wanted a cleanly shaven face. So Curt lathered the shaving mug and brush and got out the razor to shave his dad. The old man told him how his beard grew this way and that, and how he needed to turn the razor up at one point and down at another.

After the shave, Curt dressed him and carried him to the den where the family waited. He was able to sit there for almost fifteen minutes before the joy turned to almost unbearable pain. Then his eyes filled with tears, and he asked Curt to carry him back to bed. Gently, the strong adult son gathered the frail man into his arms. Curt later said, "As I made my way to his bedroom, I recalled the night many years before when he had carried me to my bedroom after our private Christmas showing. Now it was my turn to carry him."

Tears ran down Curt's face as he nestled his dad into bed; seeing the tears, the old man pointed to a tape recorder beside the bed. Curt turned it on, and together they listened to the Bible being read. It was John 14: "In My Father's house are many mansions . . ." Silently Curt thanked God for saving him, for saving his father, for giving them those moments together, and for those times when the Lord had carried them both.

Two days later, Curt's dad passed away. But the memories are precious rather than painful, says Curt, and he gives thanks. "Because of Jesus, whose birth we celebrate on Christmas and who died to save those who believe in Him, I know I will see my father again. And what a family reunion that will be."

Christ requires me to give.

He requires me to wash feet.

It amazes me to realize that
Jesus even washed Judas' feet.

What an awesome Savior to wash

the feet of His own murderer.

KIRK FRANKLIN

45

His Blue Skies Are Gone

It should have been a pleasant summer's afternoon in Clearwater, Florida, for ten-year-old Eric Miller. School was out, and he was playing at a friend's house, waiting for his mom to pick him up. When she didn't show up, Eric grew curious, calling home but getting no answer. His misgivings increased when a police officer showed up, asking for him. The officer, saying little, drove Eric to his house and left him in the back seat to peer out of the window at the yellow crime-scene tape.

"My imagination was running wild," recalls Eric, "and each minute that passed felt like an hour. Just when I didn't think I could stand it any longer, a detective approached the police car. I could see distress on his face, and by the time he got to me, I was in tears."

"Your mother is deceased," said the man.

"Does that mean she's dead?" asked the ten year old.

"Yes," replied the officer.

A surge of rage flooded Eric's heart, and it continued for years. He was furious with God, angry with the man who was later convicted of the murder, and at war with the world. His older sister, Michelle, a college student, tried to raise him, but as Eric entered his teen years he was out of control, drinking and doing drugs. By the time he was a freshman in high school, he was involved with girls, playing football by day and partying by night. When his sister tried to admonish him, he looked into her eyes and said honestly, "I don't care. I don't care if I live or die."

The police called Michelle at about 3 a.m. on the morning of her wedding. Eric had left the wedding rehearsal dinner the night before, gotten drunk, and had been arrested for driving under the influence. He was in jail. She decided to let him stay there until the morning, and at 8 a.m., she showed up at the courthouse, an unexpected stop on her way to the wedding chapel.

She was furious with Eric, but she also remembered the countless prayers she had offered on his behalf. Only two days before in her devotions, she had asked God, "Please let something happen in Eric's life that puts him on the path you want him to follow."

"Could this be it?" she wondered. "It's a strange answer to prayer."

But it was God's answer, for as he had sat on the cold floor of his cell that night, frightened, surrounded by criminals, Eric had started praying. And God had made a jailhouse visit. When Eric walked out of the courthouse that morning, he was a different person. By the time his sister had returned from her honeymoon, Eric had decided to attend the Torchbearer's Bible School in Holsby Brunn, Sweden. From there, he sent a letter to the man, imprisoned still, who had murdered his mom. Eric forgave him and shared with him the Gospel. Today, Eric is in Bible college preparing for ministry.

"I'm lucky to have had a loving sister," Eric says. "I could have asked for none better. I just thank God for putting her in my life and for her unconditional love."

The Lord God has given Me the tongue of the learned, that I should know how to speak a word in season to him who is weary.

ISAIAH 50:6

CAN'T YOU HEAR?

Judy Bennett thought she'd never hear her husband say, "I love you."

It's not that he wasn't trying. The problem was her ears. Judy, born deaf, had lived in a world of silence all her life.

"We could never have conversations in darkness," said Bruce. "In the car at night, for example, we had to leave the dome light on. We could only communicate when she could see my lips, for Judy is an excellent lip-reader."

But Bruce communicated his love in other ways. He had fallen in love with her when others, feeling awkward, had sometimes avoided her. He had learned to speak slowly so she could read his lips, and he had learned to understand her slurred and indistinct spoken words. He had introduced her to his friends, and he had embraced hers. He had learned all he could about deafness and had buffered her in difficult situations, always seeking to put her at ease. Bruce had encouraged Judy in her career, proud to tell others she assembled jet engines in an aircraft manufacturing plant.

He had also included her in his career. Bruce was the children's pastor at Rejoice Free Will Baptist Church in Owasso, Oklahoma, and the church members there never avoided or ignored her. She had instantly become a part of their family.

The members at Rejoice had also helped raise the $40,000 that Bruce and Judy needed when doctors told them that a new medical breakthrough might enable her, against all odds, to hear.

In July 2000, Bruce and Judy traveled to Kansas City where Judy had a cochlear implant surgically inserted into her right ear. Shortly after, they sat anxiously as a technician turned a series of dials and knobs. Suddenly, for the first time in her life, Judy began hearing sounds. Beeping noises in her earpiece. The humming of machines. The chirping of birds outside the window. The falling of footsteps on the floor. The sniffling of a nose. The clicking of a computer keypad. Her eyes registered amazement.

It was Bruce who spoke the first words Judy had ever heard. For weeks he had secretly been planning what he would say: "The love that's inside my heart today," he slowly said, "will never change, and it will never fail. I love you with all my heart."

Judy's eyes glistened in amazement. She rubbed her face with trembling hands and gazed back at Bruce through tears of joy.

"Wow," she said. The sound of her own voice shocked her. "I can hear myself," she exclaimed. "I can hear my voice. I can hear you."

And the next week, as Bruce and Judy drove away to celebrate their sixteenth wedding anniversary, they turned the dome light off.

I AM HERE

When missionary Trula Cronk first arrived in India, she was surrounded by starving children, filthy conditions, swarms of insects, and hearts drained of the last drops of hope. She was dismayed by the ocean of human need she saw and suddenly felt helpless to do anything. Then an older missionary pulled her aside.

"No one can do all that needs to be done," said the older woman. "No, not even all of us put together can do it, so each of us must go about the task given to us, thanking the Lord for allowing us a little bit of the blessing that comes from serving others."

Her words sank into Trula's heart.

The woman continued, "You will never add one bit to your ministry by pulling a long sad face. Rejoice in the Lord. Obey Him by fullfilling your own calling, and let the Lord take care of the rest."

That advice helped Trula serve the Lord for the years to come.

∞

Let us lean upon Jehovah's strength;

let us joy in it by unstaggering faith;

let us exult in it in our thankful songs.

CHARLES HADDON SPURGEON

Thank You, Jesus

Reading, spelling, and grammar didn't come easily to Suzanne Franks. She struggled immensely to understand the lessons. "My older brother was smart," she says. "He's the one who always got the good grades without trying. I studied hard, but I was always struggling with my grades."

On a particularly disheartening day in the fifth grade, Suzanne opened her report card to discover a large, ugly D alongside the subject of reading. She had applied herself diligently, and was hoping for a C or even a B.

A feeling of shame and discouragement swept over her, and she might have given up, but for a Bible verse the Lord gave her. She had recently learned this verse, Isaiah 40:31, at youth camp where it was sung as a chorus:

Those who wait on the Lord

Shall renew their strength;

They shall mount up with wings like eagles,

They shall run and not be weary,

They shall walk and not faint.

Armed with that verse, Suzanne found a tutor to help her, and she pressed on. By the end of the year, she had turned her grade into an A-minus.

Amazingly, Suzanne later earned her Master's degree in linguistics and became an English teacher and an editor of Christian literature for her denomination.

Her favorite verse is still Isaiah 40:31. "When I lean on that verse, as I do constantly," she says, "I'm leaning on the Lord. And when I rely on the Lord, I'm leaning on a shoulder that never weakens and resting in arms that will never let me fall."

HE LOVES YOU MORE THAN YOU'LL EVER KNOW

The steadiest and sturdiest people in the world are those who walk with God through faith in Christ Jesus. Those who draw daily from His love. Those who begin and end the day in His presence.

Charles Spurgeon, Britain's "Prince of Preachers," once admitted: "I have had to lean on the bare arm of God. It is a grand sensation. An arm of flesh loses all charms after we have once leaned on the greater power."

Friends are vital to our lives, and we can't do without them. Through them, God can work wonders.

We also can lean on God directly. He blesses us when we share with Him our deepest needs, loves, hurts, and pains.

There is tremendous hope in our friendships and in our relationship with God. Consider these amazing blessings:

- Our friends can pray for us when we can't pray for ourselves; God can answer prayers and meet our deepest needs.

- ~~Our friends can love us through difficult times; God is a friend who sticks closer than a brother.~~
- Our friends can give us their time; God is with us always, even to the end of the world.
- Friends can gather around us, giving us their warm presence and their hugs; Jesus can live within our souls.
- Friends can empathize and sympathize; the Lord Jesus Christ can read our thoughts and plumb the depths of our hearts.
- Our friends can give godly advice; Jesus can direct our steps.
- Our friends can lift our spirits and encourage us through the Holy Spirit; Jesus can make us soar on eagle's wings.
- Our friends give us happiness; Jesus gives us joy.
- Our friends can make a day go better by leading us to look to Jesus; Christ gives us life more abundant and life everlasting.

SAFEHOUSE OUTREACH MINISTRIES

Located in downtown Atlanta, Georgia, for over eighteen years, SafeHouse has impacted many lives through faith, hope, and love in action.

SafeHouse's Urban Center provides over fifteen services to diverse culture groups, including offering referrals to drug rehab centers and finding employment and permanent housing for those who need it.

The Family Resource Center encourages young women to carry their pregnancies to full-term instead of aborting their babies. The Center offers a mentoring "mom" for the women to "lean on." The women can also attend parenting classes, take computer courses, and receive job assistance and GED help to increase their self-confidence.

The Revolution ministry offers a home to youth who are considered outcasts by society. These young people are surrounded by a "family" who exemplifies love, mercy, and the grace of Jesus Christ.

YouthReach America provides a safe place for at-risk middle school students to go while their parents are at work. They receive love and attention while completing homework assignments, having daily devotionals, and hanging out.

SafeHouse also holds Block Parties to serve Atlanta's most needy communities. During these events, hundreds of teams from surrounding countries come to the Urban Center for a week of helping others. SafeHouse is striving to hold similar outreaches in every major city across the nation and around the world!

For more information about SafeHouse,
call 1-800-900-4787, or go to our Web site at
www.safehouse-outreach.org.

If you've ever had a shoulder to lean on, remember to offer yours in return to those who need it!

FROM THE PUBLISHER

What a privilege it is for us to present this wonderful book of encouragement. We are thankful to our friend Kirk Franklin and to all the others who have had a part in its creation.

During our many years of service, there have been times when my wife Marsha and I have had to lean on our fellow Christians for emotional and spiritual support. We count it an honor when we can also bless others by allowing them to lean on us. In our daily walk, we are called upon to bear the burdens of one another and to lean not on our own understanding but on God.

We praise the Lord for caring people who have reached out or who will reach out to others in times of need, and we are hopeful that this book will be a wonderful connection at those special times.

Jack Countryman

Touching Lives . . . Changing Lives

Can

I AM HERE

lean on me

H a

You're my friend, but you're a

You Can Lean On

you hear him
He's waiting just to ease your troubled mind

l l e l u j a h

my brother
you call

HE
LOVES
YOU
MORE
THAN
YOU'LL
EVER
KNOW